C000144505

The Bovine Two-Step

Rebecca Reynolds

New Issues Poetry & Prose

A Green Rose Book

New Issues Poetry & Prose
The College of Arts and Sciences
Western Michigan University
Kalamazoo, Michigan 49008

An Inland Seas Poetry Book

 Inland Seas poetry books are supported by a grant from
The Michigan Council for Arts and Cultural Affairs.

First Edition, 2002.

ISBN   1-930974-22-1 (paperbound)

Library of Congress Cataloging-in-Publication Data:
Reynolds, Rebecca
The Bovine Two-Step / Rebecca Reynolds
Library of Congress Control Number: 2002104240

Art Direction   Joseph Wingard
Design   Mat Nyenhuis
Production   Paul Sizer
                   The Design Center, Department of Art
                   College of Fine Arts
                   Western Michigan University

The Bovine Two-Step

Rebecca Reynolds

New Issues

WESTERN MICHIGAN UNIVERSITY

Also by Rebecca Reynolds

Daughter of the Hangnail

for Lynne

Contents

Seam

I should enter winter without the commonplace—
sparrows
in the city of cubes,

the trail of footmen dispatching
a stiff fall, fallen leaves, repetitive
singularities,

the winter's white-on-gold, compositions
of brick and inlay, burgeoning
privacies.

Goodnight blackbirds winging to black on black.
Here is our lengthening: a meadow of knots
behind the copse—

minus the referential, our love for that coordinate star
vs. the fracturing
and subsequent, simultaneous

featuring.
To be so intricately *there*
and never with me

(as sight will land in the saplings, and tango, eliminating
the line). She understands
an aching sabotage.

This necessitates seeing
time. An achingly blue fall. Not
as a spiral, not

as a knot. Rather as the tree identified as cherry
by some new friend, to whom
she is achingly polite,

against the slur
of the electrical. Inverted
themes recur:

her vulpine looks, the city illuminator, *paterfamilias,*
the hat-lamp in the unlit woods,
the harmony of the spheres.

I'm reading to my niece about a fox: the fox
behind the tree, the tree-leaves, probing
the rabbit hole

(as something unbroken alternates with something frittered)
inside the moon-round sky, the eve.
Minus certainty among the axes' infinite points, infinite places.

If I am not mistaken we were all writing poetry, except for Ettore, who said it was undignified for an engineer. Writing sad, crepuscular poems, and not all that beautiful, while the world was in flames, did not seem to us either strange or shameful . . .

—Primo Levi, *The Periodic Table*

The Bovine Two-Step

A woman had trained cows and bulls in a traveling act.
O garland of fury—

I was linked to extravagant organs:
the five dancers, feathered and pearled à la Josephine Baker,

the compliant dogs, who herded us, who were blessed
with these marvelous repositors of dung. *There is no object*

so foul that intense light will not make beautiful—
nature, so clotted with scat, the wild carrot, me in my dancing
                    shoes among

the most sordid and delicate of observations. A strange progress:
the body fixed to the spirit and the spirit following,

like the mammoth, discerning,
describing its own design,

the skin-flank, glimmering heart, liver-scent and hoof.
How I dreamed of it in the blossomy fog,

how I had no possessions but this dream.

Presentism

Construct a slumber house and let the leaves be guests.
Snare water in the leaves.
Drape rags on the twigs for a withered look.
Then light a red light.
Let wind drown the tree roots with fire-petals
as black-eyed Susans press
through late September like yellow births.
A fat-eye buttons the flaps.
The poet Mayakovsky said he felt like a cloud in trousers.
A little genderless . . .
although I wanted the little bobbins and tulle,
the baby, her mouth with the careful seam of Jewry,
the Lithuanian half. Rain in the light margins, so thick,
the house mottles.
Then over the inscription, a transparency / write in layers,
glitter and fly-wings, a fascicle . . .
include the autobiography, begin
they had crossed the country, both dark people,
but everyone mistook her father for the Jew and end
the cat is my muse.
Between the leaves, simultaneous threads resemble
stitching on folded moths, sequins, a stiffened blur,
the tooth in a purse (too simple and too difficult
to identify with the attic flower). No evidence
of childbirth, but envy
for the mother's snore, the garden of nectar, feverfew,
Sweet William, cave blooms. Some things
that do not need to be rewritten in her slow breath
with the lemon snapdragons.
Try rewriting the world as you perceive the thing, so far past
accuracy . . . there's the labor,
the fearful pressure at the opening. Can violence be self-
enacted, out-flicted, when you move through the frame
and beyond yourself, the spittle shape? So the edges
furl and disassemble, so the failures and the beauty are the same (o
relativist), so the details are never-ending, dusky
or light, with the small weight of trousers?
Try keeping an almanac of this.

A Lady's Manual

I dreamt I was on a journey in search of a savior (no, a *scientist*)—

then dusk transported me along the sea

where tiers of light swept the tidewater at my feet, which, like the
        Light Princess', were silk'd
and slipper'd

as if I'd stolen some other woman's skin—but also a changeling
        (I had a child with me)

and for miles the last orange sun filtered the pools, the whorls of
        conch, colloidal fish, anemone,
surf-eaten spines and kelp

and the seashore, also a desert

and together we saw no one, but so much did I require this
        scientist, or *man of learning,* I had
become a Sympathetic Creature,

weightless and wristed in thin lace, not of the sea but having the
        power to grant sea-wishes by
whatever was compelling me

i.e., the wishes of fishers and the liberation of nymphs

and other acts of vanity

with beauty and the mysterious infant as my props, forgetting for
        an instant the natural world, my
human lover and me in the sheets, asleep

when I entered the scientist's home, in the midst of a celebration,
        warmed by coppery lamps and
stemware, and guests

who toasted his most recent discovery, though little did I

understand of physical chemistry—yet
instantly

he fell in love, though he kept his love concealed and gave me a
room

in which to sleep, because of the child and my evident exhaustion,
the sense that I was in some kind
of distress due

to the transparency of my skin, pellucid, sea-like

and because I was, suddenly, inspiring rapture

though I knew, too, that I was dangerous, a curse, something about
me was deceitful

in the wraith's disguise, that I had the desire to make him wander,
to lose conjecture and thus all
reason, propelled

without method in the aftermath, where we set off

through the virgin woods, until all the woods were aflame

and we came to a valley beyond the woods, without knowing what
lay on the other side, and the
infant had disappeared

and the *man of learning,* discovering my aspect, met with a terrible
fate, and the rest—

the yellow thickets, my vanishing—

you could surmise

the assumption of music and lamentations, the incessant lute. Such
were my conditions, to comply

with the empire

virtually the whole of my existence, though I was not the singer, nor
        would I have foreknowledge
of the song.

Fetter

They had brought for my remark (signing) what I perceived
a Little Book, all caps, dashed off
in a strange haste (as in the fire of our issuance), a left
formation (so to speak) regarding
the shape of a journey,
or some importance thereof, a budding dark,
though the reader had blinders
so it could not be discerned—perhaps a horse had worn
those shutters—was I being led
into some abyss? The text in abeyance, where the sun had
marvel, alternate hue, dusk to purple,
a sweetness sucked from the pulp, the sun itself
pollarded on the hill crest (indecipherable)
so the eye devises
bones in the shape of letters, or vice versa. Then
a pool in the garden, the garden
in the book, loved ones superimposed . . .
as suddenly when I'd have asked of my god (quite certain) had not
a little dyspepsia confused with an air pocket
scumbled my serenity. The space
inside, reduced to a mute beauty, lilies
still indiscernible in the boxwoods, like a faint bell, echoing . . .
the headlessness of a mantle, or a sky
filled with cups. We could be anywhere:
in the lime orchard—
Deception was my Good Guide.

Door No. 1

The adverb is not your friend
says the writer of thrillers, but toss that in, errant,
for the darkness accumulates so thrillingly
(priming love and death), wherein

we have to plug the mind's meticulousness
(i.e., the exchange of gifts,
trade vs. warfare) and give ourselves
again and again to the bearers,

granting the evidence therein.
Oh *him* in a crisp tux with carnation. Your most obdurate flower
        arrives

wavering between logic and the brain's ignition.
Do nothing adverbial.

Flexagon

a paper crown with flaps, may be used
for telling fortunes

In a blue, French room
the sister without a face turns to the woman who
specializes in divining. As the ex-lover in the street
below passes from shadow into the deep vector of a lamp.
Then call *her* sister. Light from the diviner's eye,
a meandering. What is the future of thought? Our children
finger our wedding gowns and remark on their smallness,
the smallness of our bones. How could the officer fit
in that suit? The size of his waist—so slim, so feminine!
Yet a man back then could be so very matter of fact.
First this happened, then that. A fixed rodeo, the girl
on the sun deck gathering rays in the broad anchors
of sun, no temporal confusion there (note the afflatus
of spirit, animal magnetism, the body ringed by
phenomena, in-streaming powers broached over tea,
despite the polite rocking). So the future gives rise
to the swoon of yarrow pinned to her wedding hair, to the
sparrows of conception, to the vanishing point, the odor
of a bread belt, hypotheses darkling in the remote space
between "if" and "so" after the most humbling of events.

The Thing that is so Small and Round

Like is to like:
the small globe is evident silver,
a silver world, the word, the thing-to-the-thing,
my worth, the worth of gold,
mouth-tones of bells.
I am exceeding, exceedingly cool.
In raptures of cold, ice and water snake
where the sun is suckling
and the cold has a sound
with nothing there, and nothing
not there,
unless there
are calamitous silences
and calamitous deafnesses.
A mutism.
Say it; the dancing
made of us a lytle thing
within calamities.

Match

. . . dreamt of primordial things, bugs in a small whorl,
candles on the mice's backs.
Link this
to a feeling of uselessness, the loss of a face.
Though everything is duplicitous
and comes back in,
what comes in is
singed. The figure
could be stripped
while folding the air around herself . . . in
the little town of lead dwellers,
though wakefulness is wise.
The chill is so severe
the light slips down, without color
(think sun, the beams
unlink) though a word
is not domesticated, like the sun
and in this glare
I would transcend the patterns of morning
though I too am aware of daily things,
of their recurrences,
till something opens, flowering.

Eye-Painting

miniature paintings of the lover's eye were presented as gifts

Windblown,
the famous snow, the seer's moon,
the felt whir of wheels on the snow street,
thin domestic battles,
the sound of the universe. Saint Paula,
pursued by a youth,
ducked inside a church and sprouted a beard,
and so was saved. I, too,
sprout beards. Mornings, I pluck,
impatient, vain,
thinking I should let it go, like wild aster.
What of snow, the wild nor'easter come upon us?
and such light things, forbidden?
I would show my eye, alone, glassed
in the Victorian setting of a pin,
an eye, a painted tress,
presented to a man, a woman . . .
what of the paper marking this—
the wind in a mad hop
when the blanket on the roof begins to slip,
irrevocable. The frenzy
of a piercing cynic.
Let her open her coat,
the word touches something inside.

Anchoress

This shewing was quick & lovely & hidouse & dredfull,
swete & lovely . . .

—Julian of Norwich

Also in the sense of sweat—
it's here the arbitrariness opens.
The sun comes out from the cloth
(so often, substituting light for feeling),
a day-by-day similitude.
I lunch in my coat, frown, count
sugars, replicate
a small act, like folding leaflets, pray
as if there were a space in which to speak
and then a vehicle, thus
to make small whispers.
What physical form? In the flesh
silence and the world are vast, the air
a knitting place. This—
invisible
         though local, concrete, electric—
linked
         in preparedness
like ice-chairs waiting for the ladies on the frozen river,
or the shoemaker's last,
or the trace of her boot among batches of snow-dust,
or a pair of thinly seamed gloves,
each gesturing the other,
            finger to finger
        in the coolness, in the prison
of their small murmurs.

Jupiter

A retriever loveth me.
We light candles. The month is flat and human,
without bone. And we are pallid
in the too-white
luminosity of snow.
And I have troubles
I'd rather not discuss, and hope
to be saved by a hound or a lady,
along with the maidens in the backdrop of my scenic thermometer.
One is waking to a lively sort of dream-state
for a thousand years,
and one lies sleeping.
Candle-Lite
Fragrance De-Lite.
A fraction bigger and it would have turned into a star
and our solar system would have had two suns.
But as it is, I lie with the snow dog
who is keeping arrows by the lake
in the place where the cypress leaves are forever falling.
And we are waiting for the Great Cloud.

Moon Hotel

The neighbors, deft and silvery,
solicit ice.

I'm watching beneath the surface.
Lucky for me, lucky for me

the earth keeps busy, molten at the core.
A fist

of incessant burning,
consumption and kindling, kindling

and waste. My breath is sealed in my bounds.
The lovers come for valentines,

mid-month, in red packages.
And here

we are ecstatic, planning trips to sphery places
for our Free Gift.

That gift makes all the difference. Induces
the Immediate Mystery

so my eagerness forgets the here & now.
And across the world,

the orphans, too, consider suckling.

House Flora

Proliferation is abject:
wisps of retriever and cat, mint-stalks

filched from the garden with wild aster—
as in a spell. The least angle calculates

the fascinum: nos. of exceedingly small animals,
a spider with six eyes,

a lemon wheel, a pinch of thyme or duckweed,
when the tiniest adjustment thrills the scenery

like snow.
To burrow, or conceal one's body by closing the eyes

(as in hope's invisibility),
like the actress on TV who wants to be a size zero, gradually

cease to be distinguisha . . .
so my lover loves me for my vanishing nature   *for my*

l air
h   *air . . .*

and on the floor, a vulgar mulch.
Fuck silk and the hand-sewn leaves.

To re-build the dispersed arbor:
stirrups of a thin musculature, of vine, un-

articulated pinnings, a thistle
for the ear's Chartres, plus a lot of errata, and thorns

I'll gather in the hatched egg-cups, blue
with pearl dribble.

To disburse
is not to disburden, but to lick

the cat's ear, like this:
descend

into small motherings. And these
are mundane: the waxen "o" of the doctor's quick thermometer

in and out of my ear, like *this;*
or the needle nosed in by the quiet phlebotomist—

to relinquish company for the local tufts,
the exhalations, the spongiole,

when the land springs up.

A Backward Oracle

No, I do not think so. The thought
is seraphim, an emanation that refunds itself
into the
approximation of waters, like much incipience,

the melon's sugaring bruise
or something within the symmetry of
Minsk and Pinsk,
or the Shakers' sisterly and brotherly wings, the men
and women in tandem who touch
thread, thresher, rue,
until one day the Spirit answers little Hannah.
It is the tree of life, she says. Then dictates
cross-hatching on a paper field.

There's a good day for every bad . . .
The mind bundles autumn with spring, invents
the apple-peeler, trundle, and dumb-waiter,
even has a little cash left over, for of all things, a Cadillac.
And though evil depletes us
work replenishes: freeing a moth, or learning
penmanship through words like "Ortolan" and "Quince"
(what use "Xerxes" but to write home about the battles
when "home" is "the world"?).

Something deep and orange at the curb,
a leafless flower with a hairy stem—
a peripheral note . . . the illustration of a weed, knots
of bachelor's buttons and daisies, beardsflower, summer pods
and brush from the pine

like some toppled broom or Porcupine's Delight.
Each flower a "w," a jester's hat,
a survey for the inveterate Xerxes among the Ortolans.
And sometimes the neighbors have reported a nervous light
emanating from the trees—
though there's nothing here but my eyes.

The Parched Thread

I can make so few long-winded sentences without bowing to the
           long wind.

I was caught incompleting a task, for the work was so . . .
           enervating, and we
lacked conviction, thus a labor was lost with this conviction of a
           lack and a lost labor, thus

the drowsy terribleness . . . and getting caught
like a girl on her long white bed touching herself, until she creaks

on the thin, painted string of youthful rust (the girl on her long,
           white bed
painted with a small "O" inside her mouth). Our spines unleaven
           the feather mattress, and soon

we have to remove the TV from the bedroom to reclaim ourselves,
           slip the laws
off our bodies, where the laws are almost pretty, computer chips,
           set with yesses and no's,

1 O 1 O
the moral universe comes down to this, like sea birds

coming down to the bottle-glass horizon, smallifying.
Covetousness is a sin—

wouldn't it be better to measure our acts by kindness? or is it so
           impossible to prove
(and proof is measure) or do we need commandments, thus to be
           commanded

such and such is sinning, thus
to enlighten ourselves in the light, white thrall of the attic room?

The Object without the Interpretation

In the woods that become a meadow there is a noticeable blossoming from which we grow smaller and smaller in the evermore mysterious *whatness* with the Lythrum and Monarchs the body visible in the thin grass the clock ringing the birds out front on cue

and upwards men retire to red-lit rooms or swim through glass buildings with a smear of scotch to gossip about mergers so the event is the cooperation of "infrastructures" and that is where I come in leaving the sentence half-finished hard on myself for working the day job thinking the *you* should bear some affinity to the object of love but what of the aspen tree and the round star? what of the breath the confessor the private? what of the sentimental what of the O? *So many people possess the objects of their belief* and the rich man who shut his doors on the world dreams of hurtling into space—

headlong, eternal, the wilds of bitterness before him.

Little Rivers

A girlhood opens on the dream of a horse, the horse
leaping from an overhang into a frosted pool,
horses in snow, in statues, in the iciness surrounding the newel
        posts,
in the snow-burdened trees, a solid, remote history
in the redness of winter, the nap of ghosts in the light's bottom.
And each of us, whether knowingly or not
draws each breath
through the spit and tendons of those who are
suffering, despite euphony among dishcloths, incantatory jokes
mid-memory,
or a sound that is suddenly relevant, but also imagined,
graphing the willow branch, when the ice cracks gingerly
beneath the surface, perforated with engines and steam.
The ice is thin and papery, the children amphibious, here
in the census-drawn depths.
There's the tale of seven brothers who go fishing,
who, counting each other one by one, forget to count themselves,
        so assume
they are missing one . . . and the missing one
floats beneath the surface with a stare
fixed on the snowy lips of the bank like an inner I
who neglects the public
for the hush of an atmosphere,
the cool suburban visitors with fins,
the thrilling constituency.

The Snowflake Scarf

Or how we conceive of them. Agents of comparison,
the tiniest mote that nectars with the fruit-eating birds
in labor and in stealth, beneath the trees like apples (no, a breast),
　　　　the garden
hung precisely between tips.

She takes a candle to the cool lung of the room, before
the opposite interrupts
and the trees are hung with winter fruit, which doesn't appear
symmetrical. She lives among flares:

the mirror at the wrong altitude, a face
held wrong by its hook, the porcelain smudge, the dead
flowerpot on the stoop (flash of intense sun on the icy lot,
picking up another fifth in the Midwestern February), and nothing
　　　　left

but to plot a red garden from the catalog of tulips
(purchase bobbins for purposes of holding small amounts of yarn
　　　　for multicolor patterns) . . .

There is desire in jurisprudence *I began this work to commemorate*
the error of cities　I dreamt my boss called me a Jew,
my father's beauty on the tablecloth spread with stones
where we bet on the numbers;
we have graying sleeves and a servant's heart.

The Hanging Gardens

In labor and in stealth beneath the trees, like apples (no, tears)
like a breast   she's heavy as the dove-shaped loaves

a situation can't be called either / or
as an incident veers

and loosens in the polar, iridescent loveliness
and the beams walk out from the building

and the gills cling to her forearms. She sells fish:
at night the mica whorls down the drain and back to those regions

where coastlines fog and the father
arrives home to the mothered apartment   and a shoe

drops on the threshold   and all the shoes
fall in the shimmering   innovations in form

revise the seas   gills eddy below the surface
illustrations of starfish survive *as a particular feature of the period*

and a monkey prepares a breakthrough in the buried gardens
with the hummingbirds, nectaring

in the brown estuary (perpetual frescoes)   the idea of a drowned,
          molten flower.
The life undersea is lurid and the other life

is a rude escarpment
as the rustle of a bag disrupts our office work

and a voice stops for snow.

Sea Legend

... intensified in the steamy upper light, as if the sun were hanging
        and necessity ...
    my mother never finished her sentences, we were always
        supplying
words

in the map of a state a road dips south for miles, and at the ocean
    comes to an abrupt end, or
swerves

back   in the snowbanks of thought
hair

isn't particularly beautiful   our love for them
    almost always imperfect but who says these things
wherein

we admit to our knowledge   my mother's sentences
    going down to the sea in sea baskets, following
the remains

coming up at night in the water, the reflection of clouds
    on the foamy tides, the neoprene black
tarped

between continents, the coasts sugared with snow   by the
    fence in the snow-light yard, where the catkins purl on the
arms

of the pussy-willow   a feather survives the ride
    down from the snowy branch, a dead
blue-bottle

bobs belly-up on the sill   and the silent part finishes
off-season, in the salt

occasional
like birds at a hayride, like a visitation.

Biz

The rebirth figured in the afterbirth with the layings-on of words
the image / text / music collide
in towns off the coastline, fringing the map
Loveladies Shipbottom Wildwood

a girl sings *Tomorrow* on her way to school / this morning /
outside
a student fingers her foamy ball, the TV—
about technology and organs

so the plum gardens beneath our breasts just open and close all
            night . . .

and then, on my way to work, the windows
heaped with detergent and pink cans, a millennial star dust
beaches in the powdered sun, or coils in sleepiness

behind the glass, like millions of cats
            who wandered from the hill town seeking
lakes of water-milk on the black streets beneath the trestles
beneath

thick retaining clouds   and somebody's *higher power* is fixed on
            the cloudless page

with any variety of euphonic lines suspended

The Letter and its Sound

. . . hummingbirds in the brown estuary . . . though the creatures
        could be removed
by fiat, by the wishes of the priest-kings

(the political system was probably feudal or theocratic)   and
        somebody'
s
something

is already on my page! and little girls, false with desires,
turn into slipknots and buckles, in coltish forms   so a shyness
        curls

in the drawer
of bleached entanglements.

The history of the middle class—
a woman could be endowed

with a moon-colored girdle and bend in the stone windows
and all I'd remember is *elastic*

and the physics of mirrors, and she'd watch me becoming a little
        blurred
like the inside of a diamond (except I know it's my goddamned
        sight

this time, and start again from the vantage point of nowhere)

the house is my father
the height is my mother

and the dead night surrounds us with owls and snow.

The Letter A

. . . from underneath the tents
whereby the joist slips out of the frame   and settlers begin to
          migrate

from the lath   then so-and-so arrives . . .
first they are foraging, then forging   then they plant the gardens
          in the houses

with a marble
interiority   banana plants flopping for light like workers

to which we are insensible   here are the clean ruins
of those who had been lectured to, especially   still

with this bone of history and blindness, blindness
and no sight   no insight   stones chucked in a leftover
          spot

they, too, seem to pine for value, less the imposition of beauty,
a recurrence, echo, digging—

an encampment? the courtyard littered with cots and medicines,
the emperor's abandoned pallet,

the dead moonbeam   to make symbolic ruses
of an echo AND a discovery   why *here* in any physical sense?

why not Iceland? in the turf huts? there
we'd be one with the sod   the inside of earth /

the outer ring   the spheres alternating labor with fire
(from what I've seen of fire)

until we get caught in circles there   in the laws of peasants and
          diggers
as the spirit orbits the pole of the body

feeling occasional;
or I could be a leaf in the greenery.

The Muscles are Roomed

where *bone* is a word, everything is just words:
trucks, or reason

in the aftermath of words. Her father,
one foot in the grave, deflects
his camera eye

from her mother's green, grave blanket
which dips
beneath the gruff, luminous turf.
Here is the park and the sparrows

unreeling. Allow
the sequence of events to change:
elsewhere, two boys
plunge over their father's heart.
In the foreground, the mother / aunt / sister / uncle weeps

so far from us it looks
like a movie: a bleached rock,
the khaki hills,
further allusiveness where the honey reigns.
Unreal. Where the honey reigns
springs sweetness and springs bitterness,

the sweet and bitter herbs.
The tribes who wandered through the desert grieved
for the house, for the doorway blooms,
and the house would dream of its grapes and wells,
of a throat, a petal,
water
where the insects hummed

a discrete quantity of water, altho' the bedrock could not
investigate its own
fissures, for our participation in
the event
is the event.

The lucid C in the field is a thumbnail of moon
over the house,
over the lilacs and catalogs. Ah, the leaves

reverberate, home furnishings
are red this month
red this
red that
with a touch of faux marbling. We're composed
of repellent molecules, hence
the chemist notes that we're repulsive.
Thus one could only loosely believe. Death
is a river. Last month

the town in the flood plain went under.
So did the hogs. A film crew
shuffles through rooms
where surfaces cohere
in thin, black tips
until the camera becomes us
dreaming of solitary nightgowns, despite
the inordinate intricacy of a mating dance
between dragonflies, 30,000 lenses in their eyes,
and the male, when mounting the female,

will scoop out the eggs of previous mates
while the notes waft
here comes the bride.
A lank tune fumbles between
the humidity of colors
in the cloud-cut rafters, an equation
threads from a music-box: the slender form is propped
on a needle, while the ring
naps on a pillow, and little tears
unlock a finite world. Regards
to the turquoise sea, regards to the palm birds.

Primer

1. Where the language sets out to instruct, disregard the
     instruction.
2. The text neglects you, the lettering is hair. The birds
3. roost on the banks like fagged extras
4. in the wake of lambs. Maybe sound
5. fills the seventh day.
6. *The wind does not designate an object but substitutes for its*
     loss.
7. The body wavers
8. between rims, always suggesting itself, as it settles
9. in the wool and the musk. The heft, I accept,
10. (we were forewarned) without guessing its loves. Nor
11. is the formatting always deliberate. Indeed,
12. there's so little for me to decide
13. when the original typeface recurs like a state flower.
14. And daily, I spend so much time at the machinery, sustaining
     the millionaires
15. who don't even know it, or help with the words.
16. Then the software insists I am writing a letter, or worse,
17. an outline. So the format is maintained, albeit arbitrarily. I'm
     not sure
18. there's any more freedom in the *Jeffersonian blueness*
19. buttering the sky behind twigs
20. on the tips of inflorescence. Each variant, underscored,
21. so no one gets caught with their pants down, so to speak,
22. for crimes against spelling. Although
23. I would love that deviance: a woman, thick
24. with unexpected beauty. Not what *they* would call beauty.
25. *X openly calls for a writing that no longer yearns for the unified*
     sigh.
26. O Maple Tree.
27. O New Jersey.
28. Today the mechanic shows me the clean
29. brain of my transmission. My period begins. The robins
30. are mute as a rash of forsythia. What prescience there is
31. pales amid
32. the perforations of a land
33. ghosted with iron smiths and magnolia.

Flatus

The drilling stops me from work all morning.
I should read the Collected Poems of X.
They're fixing a leak in the gas line.
In the first dream, I discovered a woman at the end of the river.
In the second dream, a fashion doll had peed in her pants.
There were two fashion dolls, and no one had changed their
        underwear for months,
and they were practically dying—
because no one had changed their underwear. So I had to perform
        CPR.
I had to breathe into their teensy, fashion-doll lungs
until one popped awake and said, *now what shall we do?*
(For one of the dolls was the spokesperson for the two.)
        Meanwhile,
the cats had walked all over my bladder.
We have four cats.
In the first dream, I had to walk for miles through yellow
        underbrush to get to the house
by the river. There were monkeys in the trees, the trees were yellow,
        pea-yellow
against the sky. There were no phone lines. The sky, also yellow,
        looked hot because of its
yellowness. But the house was cool. And when I arrived, I saw the
        house had been built from
trees. Branches framed the windows, and the twigs
stuck out like hooks for tea towels, cups, and swatches of herbs.
The woman kept pots of dried roses, and the rose petals
had dropped across the round, oak table in a red pool.
Everything had been used and re-used. The woman was living in
        her own history.
Something I might do.
Except I buy things new. If only we knew what was important,
        that is,
sickness, and poverty, and dying. A younger Stevens writes
the Pine-tree sweetens my body / the white Iris beautifies me. Now
can you imagine a guy saying that under normal circumstances?
        A straight guy?
The white Iris beautifies me.
Overwhelmed suddenly with mothers and heat. Look ma, I'm
        turning into a flower!
And the older Stevens writes, *We are the mimics. Clouds are*

pedagogues. The air is not a mirror but a bare board. As if he
feared all along that the words were only a ruse, except that some-
thing, something had inflated him. The air, too, still an aspect
of intelligence, beauty self-emanating but beyond us, utterly beyond
us, a source of understanding or a bare board? Intelligence of the
palpitating world *and for what, except for you, do I feel love?* Then
sleep *(except for you)* the rhythm of words, the unwavering
initiating sun, possibilities of truth, yet unmatched, minus the
constant after-image of the sun—to *now what shall we do—*
perturbed by the poet for being so consistent, invited and invaded
by the iris, though it might, it might be true. I'm living in this house
in New Jersey on the dog-worn grass. There is gas in the sky.
The vines out back have overtaken the arbor, and the language is
about thin air, a sort of dying and waking and dying again, *except
for you.*

Pitch

The cat accidentally sings through her throat
as some things, sleeping, sing.
The woman under *insufficient ether*
felt herself   directly under God's foot, tied to His lightning
and bended [sic] to His angles. On TV
the fictional officers compel grief.
Their lives are magnificent! Compared even
to the peacocks and the hatchlings,
to the ground flower, the lavender-white tree. Meanwhile
insurance refuses to cover a routine examination.
The house we rent faces a fine double cherry,
a pitted lawn, salted with papery, pink blossoms
and occasional refuse. The dreamer conceives of the little guy:
now you can find him at the corner bar
while the trees unpetal themselves
and the grackles pick,
and stems root upwards
through the dirt like throats.
An April exercise. I have no qualms
pitching dandelion in compost
though such acts contract with future pests. They come,
the ragged heads and bended stems,
with a stiff love, quotidian.

Myth

Morning / experiment: loves blue gloves, pre-dawn
smoothing the highway. *She* is a twin. Inevitable, division comes
because she is different, and regarded something the neighbor
did to her twin.

Morning / expedient burrows in a blue glove
behind the tenebrous, the word
for map-work, depth, admitting
individual associations that might have resonance in your
net, an infinite lair. A laciness, so different
if I said snow, or the drum of wind under the pre-dawn or within,
           for a barren cherry
(think of blackbirds and plums, or the blighted tree).
"We'll soon find out about *that* said the Old Queen."

As the blue divides, the twin moon goes behind a light
and the dizygotic sun issues: fire
molested with New Jersey, a whiteness, just
October now, not really snow that hovers across the long route
           south so
nothing and everything is bigger than one's self,
as cups of maple float, dog-colored
like my eyes. An industrial wall girds the enormous valley
plugged with strip malls; a white church

divides the immediate blue / morning
of all lingering darkness, the threads of earlier trees,
of the tenuous, the smoke, the limned.
My eyes? my other half clowns
my ass which interrupts the procession—
what could have been a nice little meditation as morning spangles
           into view

with a string of dividends, a string of gems the asphalt rolls up my
           forehead
(I must be tired), a blue monument (the sky?) cut by the white birds
and opals, which are static / dancing
thumbnail-sized against the distance of the northern valley,

a little lake district there, with a bear problem.
(Luckily, the neighborhood association voted against a bear hunt.)
My clogs look like sweaters with embroidered paws.
This is merely a suggestion.

And often, the neighbor molested her fire-twin and she couldn't say
        anything.
We've had thoughts, too,
not just revenge but dallying with the erotic—
the crotch in its saddle, yet not liking the echo, dip back
into a long expanse of tenebrous music, a forked theme, so
        undeniably
a piece of the country.

Nature Poem

The woman is a bear. Her kids, not expecting this
to be so, are surprised when they too develop a certain bearness:
lumbering extravagance, bushy coats,
a gross attraction to trees, a sense
that the earth is rapid, the girth
of their tongues delighting in Asian pears, in plums,
as their noses develop a flair
for night soil, ejecta.
She loves her nature, like all bears, intent
and self-involved, devoted to ablutions, lickings
and skin-care, the need to drop a stool here and there,
and hunger, hunger, so her children
follow, remembering blueberries,
and how they lost their trail when mother
kept nosing the mountain. They would put up tins
if they had the thumbs for it. But no,
it had become a given. No thumbs. No detail work.
A slicked-up hide is art. They'd make a beeline
for the hiker's pack, or a locked food box, which any bear worth its
        bulk
could rip, or crush. And so, they took to crushing stuff
while the neighbors gawked, but
mother said to pay no mind
for the neighbors would do their delicate things.

Shadow Box

We lunch in the club with gold stars. Linens unbloom,
the secretary to my left forks through red
bib lettuce. Like me,
she sees her father in the stems,
but thinks it impolite to refuse food
when the bosses are treating, so we all
end up eating of our own kind. The most vibrant meal
we have ever tasted, by the way, and say so, you know
this is *so* tender! And look! The ceiling is imprinted with leaves.
Noon stirs through the blue and white curtains.
We are all pronounced *medium* or *rare* as primly
as a twig angles through snow, or cars ribbon the distant bridge.
It is said that professional women
should wear their hair above their shoulders.
Think of growing your hair so long you need to reel it home.
Yes, it is difficult to think with all that hair. So difficult,
because, as you would imagine, the electrolytes are dammed
inside the roots, like mammals
who encounter a sudden waterfall, or rock.
Who am I? That is the question that deserves to be lopped off,
for so often one is *replaceable.* Another reason
for stashing nuts in the jowl
or eating one's immediate family. Not to be gladdened by the
        thought
of oneself in the meadow when the clover unfolds
or the burdens are ex-pressed by insects
with humorously rapid wings
that swarm your lips, fairyish, eager. Not to be impressed by
        survival,
not to be aroused by the city,
not to love an atelier,
nor to imagine that dim, sickly creator
in the hoarse blur of shadow
pitched against the wall by a candle
where the animal encounters a yellow wall
and ignores the flame,
studying the geometry of shadow. *Your sight
will wish to be in the spot exactly through a hole
placed where the light passed,* Leonardo wrote,
while the model is stripped naked
at the vanishing point.

From Latin *Insula* or Island

The coffee smoldering inside.
Something I know intimately, like being
alone, *is* being alone, without courage or presence, so
being in shadow, the safety in that,
but what is living and living with this
scrutiny, which comes and goes, the space
without an image or poetry to latch onto, here
is the stuff I throw off,
the story that erases itself each time,
or could it be the voice that is inside, in the flurry—
only propositions have sense—
"a totality of true thoughts is a picture of the world."
My father's imagination has
the beauty of a drunk's,
a picture of the world, a gully
without feeling, blue
and palatial like Crete
with some inside sounds, with the sound of chewing.
As if we voted on it, he and I, like
carpeting or flora, and now the dog is at the screen, standing
in front of winter. Something white picks at the leaves.
I am airy, keeping the thick knife of my tongue, high noon,
where Saturday diffuses. This is the best form for it,
for Saturday, for the father, humming back there
so often I have wanted to steal something inexact
from the others, from you,
finding myself with this fear
and the past was the occasion. A western light forsakes
the orange drapery. I could use a drink
this time of day, the aftermath of noon,
though the feeling is one of silence sunk into the fundament
of its own word, so the bearer is levered down, worse
because of the silence and the barest difference.
Let us cling
in that nimbus of light around Rembrandt's sitters,
to the faces we love in those paintings
because they resemble us. The man's hands
in the light, in the dark
his rings.
I know those bones, that uneasy shape.

Water Dailies

A thick foot braids the sheets where the cold air flutes
in the white perch.
The sleeper's wish: your body dries to the color of milk. A form
is permanent and cannot be altered after the original gesture.
The character is traditional.
The cat, in the squiggle of joint, displays the fine
blot of his spots. His ears are a silvered wash. And you sleep
in a single stroke. The snow's thin evidence shrivels
in the hot March day, and flies alight on the food. The flies,
called *thorid* and *humpback,* have already stuttered in the yards.
In the offices, order is a thin, black burlap
that covers the ocean of light behind the atmosphere
in the flood of returnings. Even
the music of that word, *something, something,*
the palate of *blackness,* or *under* . . .

So I End Up in the Blonde Light

Talking to my secret *you*. The puzzle I'm allowed.
Meanwhile
clarify the birds' skit and scat of predators,
the possessive grammar, the earliest blooming, the genitive case.

The software of the thighs.

A speaker conveys you. Smoke
ladders between the air and you—
it is not so small as not to be necessary. A surface proliferates.

You come with two examples
(check word order): the half-presence of milk, or sun
as the inside color. Then

the inveterate blood. Capped teeth—

the working life. A bowl
before the budless forsythia boughs that rap at the winter glass

when you come home, smelling
like the fish market, scales on your forearms

and a smoker's cough. So we end up, one night,

eating bread at the wooden table, watching cartoons
in the Mid-Atlantic light;

and the house is a grain

at the moment of our understanding
as we open into our showings,

and in this we are everlasting.

Casper

The ghost sleeps on the river, remembering pink skies,
a history one isn't exactly invited to,
and those who have forced themselves
into a language, unbeknownst to their "children's children,"
who barely touch, in seedling gestures, the woods
that deepen inexplicably, e.g.,
my grandfather in the Black Forest, before the Manhattan Project,
close enough to his birth that the soul, or breath,
meets up with the good witch, who fixed his eye.
Except it wasn't the Black Forest, but White Russia,
and the neighbors may have been wending home to their lace and
        potato dolls . . .
who will fly to their futures as if there were never a crossing
only how they do it remains a mystery. And here
you could just walk out from your despair, over the meadows
and back again, here in the new world, in our separate autumns,
always a ghost house with the somber screens and unbroomed
        walks
and the house's motherly eaves, and the lights out.
We're wishing for that cold and lonely dark
in the echo of our lunch bags, here in the unwild wilds
in the damp, blue October,
October of coral leaves and tragedies and the same operatic
        tracks—
to squeeze in through that burning,
the heart in the air, anatomically exact, discernible.

The Visible in Two Spheres Mixed

Sublime where it mingled with grief,
grief to this end . . .
a golden spire in the acrid, the overused air, used

over endless stoops, dishcloths
and other unbashful items
bunched or wrung on incessant rails,

on a rain-spattered riser below the burls of wood
and barrels, door after door,
the alleyways thinned with distance when

the Census came
and counted us, like saplings
on the blue-black street,

on the hills with the starter roses
and the established roses
and a crumple of red stones . . .

developed further, in the nature of perception,
whereas the rest
is only resemblance

and includes the animals
and everything that grows or is made,
a reflection of earlier shadows,

twigs veining the bricks like a hair net, hints
of the old country, *risolje,* close
to the solid world, or something

less terrifying than the usual,
because of what comes next.

The Human Cannonball

The wilds revise the man who rode the comet
now seeking the loveliest of men . . .

yet to hurl into the infinite /
darkness invisible by matchbox windows on the open road,

opened with human frills.
Carry him back to the thugs to the fishers

to the salt and liquid of the joint where they kindle the fire
and listen for the bell-horse in the county's sea-less embrace,

to the smell of grass and inland loam
layered with a deep rot

for which he sinks on his knees grateful
and airy an instillation,

a knoll
on the foggy moor still parceled of the hinterland.

Notes

Because they lent themselves to extraction, I should acknowledge
the following texts from which I have, very lightly, borrowed:
Emerson, "Nature;" James, *Varieties of Religious Experience;*
Julian of Norwich, *Revelations of Divine Love;* Wittgenstein,
Tractatus; and Rilke, *Duino Elegies.* Readers may notice fragments
of these works here and there throughout this collection of poems,
generally italicized (although some italicized phrases are purely
of my own invention). The Stevens quotes in "Flatus" are from
"In the Carolinas" and "Notes Toward a Supreme Fiction,"
respectively. (I apologize to both Stevens and literary critics every-
where for misreading the poet). There are less exalted sources,
too: I have borrowed from an Internet site on crochet; I have
distorted two sentences from an online, critical article on
postmodernism; and the quote from Leonardo Da Vinci in "Shadow
Box" was cited in an article by Ross Woodrow at the University
of Newcastle, "Origins in Shadow," located at the following world
wide web address: www.newcastle.edu.au/department/fad/fi/
woodrow/anal-2.htm.

Acknowledgments

Grateful acknowledgment is made to the editors of the following journals, magazines, and anthologies in which these poems first appeared, some in different versions:

American Letters & Commentary: "A Backward Oracle"

American Literary Review: "Eye-Painting"

Boog City: "Primer"

DoubleTake: "Seam"

Open City: "Casper"

Valparaiso Poetry Review: "From Latin *Insula* or Island"

Verse: "A Lady's Manual," "House Flora"

photo by Debra Van Fleet

Rebecca Reynolds was born and grew up in Washington, D.C. She received a B.A. from Vassar College, an M.A. in English from Rutgers University, and an M.F.A. in Creative Writing from the University of Michigan. She has been the recipient of a Hopwood Award, a New Jersey State Council on the Arts grant, and the 1998 Norma Farber First Book Award from the Poetry Society of America for *Daughter of the Hangnail* (New Issues Press, 1997). She works at Douglass College, the women's college of Rutgers University, as an Assistant Dean for Academic Services.

New Issues Poetry & Prose

Editor, Herbert Scott

Vito Aiuto, *Self-Portrait as Jerry Quarry*
James Armstrong, *Monument In A Summer Hat*
Michael Burkard, *Pennsylvania Collection Agency*
Anthony Butts, *Fifth Season*
Kevin Cantwell, *Something Black in the Green Part of Your Eye*
Gladys Cardiff, *A Bare Unpainted Table*
Kevin Clark, *In the Evening of No Warning*
Jim Daniels, *Night with Drive-By Shooting Stars*
Joseph Featherstone, *Brace's Cove*
Lisa Fishman, *The Deep Heart's Core Is a Suitcase*
Robert Grunst, *The Smallest Bird in North America*
Robert Haight, *Emergences and Spinner Falls*
Mark Halperin, *Time as Distance*
Myronn Hardy, *Approaching the Center*
Edward Haworth Hoeppner, *Rain Through High Windows*
Cynthia Hogue, *Flux*
Janet Kauffman, *Rot* (fiction)
Josie Kearns, *New Numbers*
Maurice Kilwein Guevara, *Autobiography of So-and-so: Poems in Prose*
Ruth Ellen Kocher, *When the Moon Knows You're Wandering*
Steve Langan, *Freezing*
Lance Larsen, *Erasable Walls*
David Dodd Lee, *Downsides of Fish Culture*
Deanne Lundin, *The Ginseng Hunter's Notebook*
Joy Manesiotis, *They Sing to Her Bones*
Sarah Mangold, *Household Mechanics*
David Marlatt, *A Hog Slaughtering Woman*
Gretchen Mattox, *Goodnight Architecture*
Paula McLain, *Less of Her*
Sarah Messer, *Bandit Letters*
Malena Mörling, *Ocean Avenue*
Julie Moulds, *The Woman with a Cubed Head*
Marsha de la O, *Black Hope*
C. Mikal Oness, *Water Becomes Bone*
Elizabeth Powell, *The Republic of Self*
Margaret Rabb, *Granite Dives*
Rebecca Reynolds, *Daughter of the Hangnail; The Bovine Two-Step*
Martha Rhodes, *Perfect Disappearance*
Beth Roberts, *Brief Moral History in Blue*
John Rybicki, *Traveling at High Speeds*
Mary Ann Samyn, *Inside the Yellow Dress*
Mark Scott, *Tactile Values*

Martha Serpas, *Côte Blanche*
Diane Seuss-Brakeman, *It Blows You Hollow*
Marc Sheehan, *Greatest Hits*
Sarah Jane Smith, *No Thanks—and Other Stories* (fiction)
Phillip Sterling, *Mutual Shores*
Angela Sorby, *Distance Learning*
Russell Thorburn, *Approximate Desire*
Rodney Torreson, *A Breathable Light*
Robert VanderMolen, *Breath*
Martin Walls, *Small Human Detail in Care of National Trust*
Patricia Jabbeh Wesley, *Before the Palm Could Bloom: Poems of Africa*